Crab Attack!

Written by John Lockyer
Illustrated by Dean Proudfoot

Aunt Bessie lives on a small island. Whenever Mum visits Aunt Bessie, she takes my sister Siti and me with her.

The first time I went there, we all rode our bikes around the island. We stopped at many houses to talk to Aunt Bessie's friends.

A couple of days later, when Mum and Aunt Bessie asked Siti and me to come on another bike ride, I shook my head. "My legs are still tired from the last one," I said.

"Mine, too," said Siti.

Aunt Bessie doesn't have a TV, so, after she and Mum left, Siti and I went down to the beach to look for shells and coloured coral. I took off my sandals and pushed my toes into the warm sand. I kicked clumps of seaweed. And that's when I saw them.

Crabs! Big, red crabs!

There were hundreds of them. They crawled over the sand and into the sea. It was very scary.

"Siti! Look!" I yelled.

Siti screamed.

The crabs came out of the trees. They were everywhere.

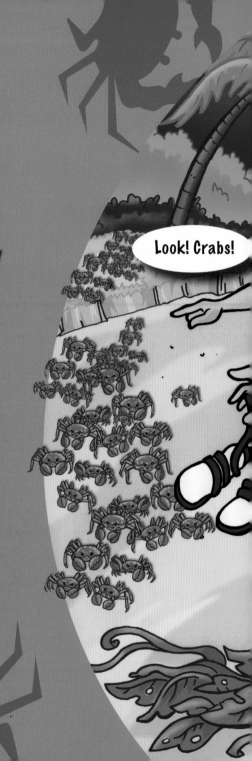

Look! Crabs!

We saw two boys along the road. They were laughing and picking up the crabs. "Where are the crabs coming from?" I shouted. But they didn't hear me.

The crabs were all around us like troops of soldiers. I shivered and climbed on a fence to get out of their way. Siti climbed up on the fence, too. The crabs were all going one way – to the sea. What was going on? Were the crabs running away from something? I knew that animals could tell if there was danger. Was there going to be an earthquake?

Now I was really scared. I wanted to scream. I wanted to go home. Siti and I jumped off the fence and ran. We ran as fast as we could, hopping and jumping over crabs.

We stopped running when we reached Aunt Bessie's front gate. There were heaps of crabs there, too. They covered the yard. They were on the steps and the porch.

I hopped and jumped up the path. Siti reached the porch and groaned. The front door was open. The crabs were inside the house! She rushed into the lounge. "Hello!" she shouted. "Anyone here?"

No one answered. I ran into the kitchen, then the bedrooms and the bathroom. The crabs were everywhere.

The crabs were all over the house. They clicked and clacked around me. It was like a bad dream. I ran into the lounge. My legs shook.

I screamed and screamed.

Then I heard Mum outside. "Lena! Siti!" Mum called. "Come and see the crabs."

"**Help!**" we shouted. "They're inside the house!"

Mum came in. She got a broom and brushed the crabs out of the way. We stood close together on the sofa. Crabs covered the floor.

Tears rolled down my cheeks. "We went to the beach . . . " I said. "I left the door open . . . They came into the house . . . Why are there so many? Why are we being attacked?"

Mum swept crabs out the door. She laughed. "Don't be scared," she said. "We're not being attacked. The crabs live on the land, and once a year they go to the sea to lay their eggs. The island is covered with them. They'll be gone in a few days."

I wiped my eyes on my sleeve. I looked at Siti. We both felt silly. Mum was still sweeping crabs out the door.

"Get another broom, Siti, and see if you can find a bucket, Lena," she said. "Bessie's still at her friend's place. Let's get rid of them before she gets home."

With Mum around, the crabs weren't so scary any more. We swept them outside. Some got stuck in corners and behind furniture. We picked them up carefully and dropped them into buckets. When the buckets were full, we emptied them out of the windows.

When the crabs were out of the house, we sat on the front steps, drinking lemonade and watching the crabs scuttle past.

Aunt Bessie came up the path, and we told her what happened. She didn't believe us. "Don't be silly!" she said, laughing. "Crabs don't go into houses."

The next morning, I was in bed listening to the crabs rattling over the rocks outside when I heard screams. They were coming from the bathroom.

Mum and I ran to the bathroom. "What's going on?" we shouted.

And there was Aunt Bessie . . . with a big crab stuck to her toe.

"See Aunt Bessie," I said. "Crabs *do* come into houses!"

17

Crab Attack! is a Recount.

A recount tells . . .

* who the story is about (the characters)
* when the story happened
* where the story is set.

Who	When	Where
	When Mum, Siti and I went to stay at Aunt Bessie's house.	

A recount tells what happens.

A recount has a *conclusion*.

▬▬▬ Guide Notes

Title: Crab Attack!
Stage: Fluency

Text Form: Recount
Approach: Guided Reading
Processes: Thinking Critically, Exploring Language, Processing Information
Written and Visual Focus: Illustrative Text, Speech Bubbles

THINKING CRITICALLY
(sample questions)
- What do you think this story could be about? Look at the title and discuss.
- Look at the cover. Do you think the girls will be safe from the crabs standing on the rock? Why or why not?
- Look at pages 2 and 3. Do you think Siti and Lena are used to biking? Why or why not?
- Look at pages 4 and 5. Why do you think Aunt Bessie doesn't have a TV?
- Look at pages 6 and 7. Why do you think the two boys weren't scared of the crabs?
- Look at pages 8 and 9. Why do you think the crabs went into the house?
- Look at pages 10 and 11. What else do you think Mum could have used to get rid of the crabs?
- Look at pages 12 and 13. How do you think Bessie would have felt if she came home and found crabs in her house? Why do you think this?
- Look at pages 14 and 15. Why do you think Lena and Siti were not as scared of the crabs when their mum was around?

EXPLORING LANGUAGE

Terminology
Spread, author and illustrator credits, imprint information, ISBN number

Vocabulary
Clarify: attacked, porch, troops, soldiers, earthquake, coral, scuttle
Adjectives: *coloured* coral, *red* crabs, *bad* dream
Pronouns: she, my, me, I, we, they
Adverb: picked them up *carefully*
Abbreviation: TV
Simile: the crabs were all around us *like troops of soldiers*
Focus the students' attention on **homonyms**, **antonyms** and **synonyms** if appropriate.